The Organist Pipes Up!

True tales of an Itinerant Church Organist.

Martin Penrose

© Copyright Martin Penrose.

All rights reserved. No part of this publication may be reproduced, stored in a retrieval system, or transmitted, in any form or by any means, electronic, mechanical, photocopying, recording or otherwise, without the prior written permission of Martin Penrose.

First Edition: 2019

Published by Sarsen Press, Winchester

Acknowledgements.

I should like to acknowledge the help of my wife Maureen, without whose help, encouragement and persistence I don't think I would have got around to compiling these articles into book form. I also owe her a great debt of thanks for putting up with nearly 35 years of the 'unsocial hours' – very rarely having a weekend off - involved in a church musician's life.

I am also indebted to my late brother Tim, who encouraged me to take an interest in music and the organ as a young lad; to the late Edwin Henning (my first choirmaster) who gave me my first lessons and to Jeremy Blandford who guided me through Grade 8 and my first diploma exam. Both of them always had a fund of amusing stories and anecdotes to tell and were the benchmark for my story telling

Index

Acknowledgements

Prelude

1. The key to playing is……..
2. Space invaders!
3. Danger money required!!
4. From Ave Maria to Hitchcock in one composer
5. The 'Bucket and Spade' organist
6. Organists' graffiti
7. Exam nerves
8. All taped up
9. Are you seated comfortably?
10. Practice makes……….
11. Friday night is music night
12. Sense of direction
13. You want what?
14. Thank you Mr Phillips.
15. How the piano kept me dry
16. Senior moment
17. Throw it away…..
18. I am so lucky
19. Themes from the classics
20. Bringing the car into the church
21. Confusion over letters
22. There's an organ where!
23. The Salmon man
24. Organs and water
25. The speed of music
26. Why we wear cassocks

27. Cinema organists
28. My Bach was much worse than my bite!
29. Music fashion
30. Manuscript rules
31. Fashions in organ music
32. Best seat in the House, or is it?
33. Pipe verses organ
34. The importance of the apostrophe
35. Pedals – the new addition!
36. Pianola – no practice required!
37. Importance of piano tuning
38. Old music copies
39. The 'reluctant organist'
40. What's in a number?
41. An exhibition of effectiveness
42. Flemish joy
43. The Patent pending organ
44. Valuable Craftwork
45. A poor workman blames his tools, surely?
46. Armed for tension
47. White out!

Martin Penrose *has been Musical Director of St Thomas' Church, Lymington, since 1998, where he has the support of a thriving choir of adults and children, a caring clergy and enthusiastic congregation. After leaving school he trained as a Journalist with a regional Evening newspaper and became organist and choirmaster at the church where he was a chorister as a child – Holy Trinity Church, Millbrook, Southampton. He also continued his musical training under Jeremy Blandford. In 1991 the pull of music became too strong and he became a full-time musician.*

He is a past chairman of the Winchester area of the RSCM (Royal School of Church Music) and is an active committee member of the local Organists' Association.

He now successfully combines being a church organist and choir director with work as a recitalist, pianist, chamber musician and teacher. Martin has performed in some of the country's leading concert venues. Recently he has recorded a third CD with cellist Philip Daish-Handy, given several concert tours, and performed with Phil, numerous times, on the prestigious P&O cruise line as the Nova Foresta Duo. In 2017 he and Phil founded the Nova Foresta Classical Players, which not only brings together a number of professional musicians who live in the New Forest, but also gives a platform to talented young musicians to play in a professional concert environment.

Martin is an avid reader and is also interested in old British motorbikes and cars. He particularly enjoys spotting when film/tv studios use the wrong age of cars in period dramas!

Martin is married to Maureen; they have three daughters and two grandchildren.

The key to playing is……..

My work as an 'itinerant' organist can find me playing for funerals all over the county.

Faced with unfamiliar instruments in strange churches one needs - in the best Boy Scout tradition - to 'be prepared'. My music bag contains all sorts of things I might require, just in case: 'Blu-Tack', elastic bands, paper clips and pins - and copies of hymns such as 'Crimond' and 'The Old Rugged Cross' that are, surprisingly, not to be found in some church hymn books.

But a job at a small church in the east of the county had me stumped. It took me nearly an hour to get there, and I duly arrived with half an hour to spare before the start of the service.

I was greeted by the churchwarden, who said she would fetch me the key to their newly installed electronic organ. Several minutes later she came back, somewhat embarrassed, and told me it was not where it should be – and the organist who had the only other key was away on holiday...

We tried to prise open the roll-top cover, but it wouldn't budge. A local handyman was wheeled in, but he reckoned it couldn't be opened without causing a great deal of costly damage. So, the vicar had to explain to the family that although they had an organist there was no instrument for me to play: They didn't have a piano or keyboard either. Fortunately, a bagpiper had also been booked for the service, so they did have some music. I duly headed for home, having earned my usual fee for a rather pleasant drive through the Hampshire countryside; as the undertaker remarked afterwards, it wasn't my fault.

However, it left me thinking that perhaps in future I should also carry a set of skeleton keys in my music case!

Space invaders!

Christmas is always a very busy time for church choirs. As well as leading the Christmas worship and performing at various carol services, there's generally carol singing to be fitted in as well.

It's a good opportunity for the choir to get out and about and provide some valuable Christian witness in the community.

At my previous church in Southampton we used to walk round the streets of the parish singing and collecting for the Church of England Children's Society.

Although it took quite a bit of organising – obtaining the correct permit to collect door to door was never easy – it was generally very well received, and the singers always enjoyed themselves.

As well as standing on street corners, we also used to visit various pubs, which enabled us to warm up and was usually fairly profitable. However, one year our visit to the pub brought proceedings to a rather unexpected early finish.

It was the early 1980s and as well as the traditional juke box, space invader machines were the latest craze in pub entertainment.

We managed to get the juke box turned off and as usual I blew the starting note on my trusty pitch pipe: However, before we started singing a space invader machine sounded a rather higher note.

Six verses of 'The First Nowell' up a major third was all we could manage that night and we retired to the Rectory for an early cup of coffee and some well-earned mince pies...

Danger money required!

The remuneration of church organists can be a controversial subject in some circles, but not many players can like me claim that they should have been paid danger money!

At the time I had no idea that the little 1950s temporary church in which I learnt my trade could have been a very hazardous place indeed. Set back from the road behind a tree screen and with a large grass paddock in front of it, it seemed quite an idyllic spot in a very ordinary suburban part of Southampton.

I played there for Evensong and other occasional services on and off for about 25 years and had no idea of the danger lurking beneath the foundations – or lack of them...

For I can only think that the builders didn't dig down very far when the church was built in 1953, otherwise they would have found all the First World War bombs and ammunition that had been dumped there sometime after 1918.

All this was unearthed after the church was closed and demolished in the early 2000s to make way for some new flats.

Construction work was brought to a halt, the surrounding houses were evacuated, and Army bomb disposal experts were brought in to make the explosives safe. Of course, by this time they had been in the ground for well over 80 years and were therefore in a very unstable condition.

At that church we used the old English Hymnal and quite often sang 'Nearer my God to Thee'. Sung to J B Dykes' tune 'Horbury' it is one of my favourite hymns: Little did I know just how close to the hereafter we really were!

From Ave Maria to Hitchcock in one composer

Gounod's setting of the 'Ave Maria', which he based on a keyboard prelude by J S Bach, has arguably become one of the world's most recognizable pieces of classical music.

But at a recent Advent Carol Service at St Thomas', Lymington, the choir performed a little known setting he wrote to the words of 'O come, O come, Emmanuel'.

Charles-François Gounod (1818-1893) was a key figure in 19th century French music, counting the great opera composer Georges Bizet amongst his pupils. He was greatly admired by the likes of Tchaikovsky, Massenet and Ravel, and at his funeral at The Madeleine Church in Paris in October 1893, the organist was none other than Camille Saint-Saëns, while the choir was conducted by Gabriel Fauré.

From 1870 to 1874 he lived in London, and during that time concentrated on composing choral music, becoming the first conductor of what is now the Royal Choral Society in 1871. The following year he wrote 'Funeral March of a Marionette' – a short piano piece which he orchestrated in 1879 and was made famous many years later by its use as the theme for the television series 'Alfred Hitchcock Presents'.

Curiously, it's just possible that he may have visited Lymington, as he is said to have had a holiday home in Milford on Sea and is reputed to have played the organ in the local Roman Catholic Church of St Francis of Assisi.

The 'bucket and spade' organist

The summer months of July and August in my mind always conjure up images of what were seemingly long, hot school holidays when I was a boy, and the 'bucket and spade' trips to the beach we took with our girls when they were children.

A favourite spot was the beach at Alum Chine in Bournemouth – generally at teatime, when the sun was less likely to burn our girls' fair coloured skin. We would drive home through Bournemouth town centre, via our favourite chip shop - always on the way passing not far from the Pavilion Theatre, where in the 1930s and 40s Percy Whitlock was the resident organist.

Percy and his wife Edna moved to Bournemouth in 1930 on the advice of his doctor: He had suffered with TB when younger and medical opinion was that the sea air would improve his health.

His first post was as organist of St Stephen's Church, but in the mid-30s he took over from Philip Dore as civic organist at a salary of £350 per year, presiding over the marvellous Compton organ in the Pavilion Theatre until his untimely death at the age of 42 in 1946.

Whitlock's duties included giving regular recitals, which were attended by many holidaymakers, radio broadcasts for the BBC, and playing the organ for concerts with the Bournemouth Municipal Orchestra, the predecessor of today's BSO.

An accomplished composer, he wrote much serious organ music – but he also wrote a considerable amount of 'light' orchestral music under the pseudonym of 'Kenneth Lark'.

One of these compositions, written in 1938, was 'Holiday Suite', which includes a charming piece named 'Spade and Bucket Polka'. A few years ago the score was found languishing forgotten in the BSO library and a recording was made of this (and other pieces) by Malcolm Riley, an organist who has also written a fascinating biography about Whitlock.

Whitlock had a great gift for writing in a very accessible style and had he lived I think it quite likely that he would have found employment writing theme music for film and television.

Organists' graffiti

Looking through my music one Saturday morning deciding what I would play before the following day's Sunday service, I came across an old album of pieces kindly given to me about 20 years before. As I flicked through the pages, I spotted some dates (something I do myself to keep track of when I have played a piece) written in pencil in an unfamiliar hand: 15/3/08 and 11/7/09 - and, of course, they referred to the years 1908 and 1909.

Quite often organist colleagues tell me that they have got rid of all their old music and replaced it with the latest modern editions, but I find older second-hand copies are generally produced in larger, clearer print and stay open much better on the music desk: However, some might suggest that it is because I am too mean to buy new replacements…

Our choir library at St Thomas contains many new music copies, but there are plenty of old ones too, dating back as far as the early 1890s. We regularly use a rather faded green Diocesan festival book, and I have often remarked to the choir that it was doubtless a rather brighter colour when it was produced in the early 1930s.

On Remembrance Sunday I generally play a piece written by my wife's late father especially for that day in November 1934, and I also use his arrangement of 'God Save the King', which was published in 1927, for the first verse of the National Anthem. By the way, he was born in 1898 and was taken as a young child to see Queen Victoria's funeral in 1901: But that's another story.

I like to think that when these old copies are used, we are 'linking hands' with musicians from previous generations.

Exam Nerves

In 1889 the Associated Board of the Royal Schools of Music was founded to create an examining body for the Royal Academy of Music and the Royal College of Music.

However, Trinity College of Music had been first on the scene, introducing their graded music exams to external candidates in 1877. From quite small beginnings, both ABRSM and Trinity exams have grown over the years to become recognised worldwide as a benchmark in assessing musical achievement.

In my time as an instrumental teacher I must have entered scores (if not hundreds) of pupils for exams, but it is all too easy to forget what a daunting process it can be.

As with any performing discipline nerves can prove a problem. Children generally take the whole business in their stride; for adults, though, who have often not undergone the exam process since their schooldays, it can be a very different story.

In the mid-1990s I was teaching a Royal Naval officer the piano while he was posted to an 'on shore' job. He was very musical and made fairly rapid progress and was soon ready to take his Grade 1 exam, which he successfully passed.

But he told me afterwards that he had found whole business so nerve-wracking that he had to sit quietly smoking a cigarette in his car and had taken the rest of the day off. And this from a naval officer who had served during the Falklands War on a ship that had come under enemy fire…

All taped up

Concert pianists and many other musicians are generally expected to perform from memory, but, like oratorio singers, the convention is that organists play from a score. As someone who finds it difficult to play more than a few bars of anything without the 'lines and dots' in front of me, this is something of which I have always been very glad.

However, playing from score still leaves one with the problem of how to turn the pages. I am very lucky in that my wife Maureen often turns pages and even changes stops for me when I am giving a recital.

But there are plenty of occasions when I have to play without the assistance of page turner. Many music publishers and editors give considerable thought to how they lay out the music, so that one has a hand available to turn the pages.

Sometimes one can get round an awkward turn by committing a few bars of the piece to memory, allowing the turn to be made when a hand is free. At other times a photocopy of a page or a few bars will solve the problem.

One particular piece, though, is particularly tricky to play without a page turner. In the famous Toccata from Widor's Organ Symphonie No 5 – a favourite of many wedding couples - both hands are in constant use from start to finish.

After one or two occasions when I was let down by someone who promised faithfully to come and turn for me, I decided to put an end to the problem once and for all.

The copy from which I still play is dated August 1984 and was produced for me by a photocopying firm in Southampton. All ten pages were reduced in size and taped together in one large sheet, just small enough to fit on most organ music desks.

However, that's not the end of the story. Pride, it is said, always comes before a fall – and the first time I used the copy someone opened the west door of the church and a strong breeze blew it off the music desk and on to the floor next to the organ console!

Fortunately, I was near the end of the piece and able to play the last couple of pages from memory. Having learnt my lesson, I have ever since made sure the copy is held firmly in place by a combination of 'Blu Tack' and bulldog clips...

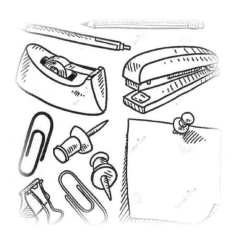

Are you seated comfortably?

Organ benches are fairly unremarkable pieces of furniture, but nevertheless they are a crucial part of the instrument. They need to be the right height in relation to the pedals and the keyboards, and to be completely stable - despite often being positioned on loose floorboards or wobbly tiles in a dark corner of the church.

At a funeral in a country church some years ago now, I arrived to find a beautifully quilted and padded cushion fitted to the organ bench with press studs. It took me quite some time to remove it (and, of course, replace it afterwards): Padding not only prevents one from playing the pedals properly (you need to be able to swivel about on the bench) but made it too much of a stretch for my short legs to reach the pedalboard.

Another local church has a modern electronic organ with a 'self-assembly' organ bench, and the members of the choir who were with me to sing for a wedding found it highly amusing that the stool made a loud squeaking noise every time I moved – despite my best efforts to tighten the joints beforehand with an Allen key.

Other perils can be caused by one's colleagues: At a church in Southampton I arrived to play for a wedding and found that my friend, for whom I was deputising, kept teetering piles of music and old hymn lists on either side of the bench. The slightest wrong move would have caused an 'avalanche' – so I removed the offending items, but was careful to reposition them afterwards, as I have a rule to leave things as I find them.

However, danger can sometimes even lurk in one's own organ loft. On one occasion I arrived at St Thomas' to find that a 'spring cleaning' party had been at work in the gallery. Everything looked spic and span and had been polished –

including the organ bench, as it turned out. I sat down to play and promptly slid off into the pedals!

Practice makes……..

For very nearly 25 years I worked as a peripatetic piano teacher at a number of schools in the Southampton area.
In that time, I must have taught hundreds of children. Some are particularly memorable because they worked hard and achieved a great deal: Indeed, one or two are now working as music teachers themselves.

But there are others who were not at all keen to practice – an essential part of learning any musical instrument. I remember one of my colleagues found it highly amusing when he overheard a boy telling me in all seriousness that he hadn't done any practice because someone had moved the piano stool into another room…

Another lad was supposed to be learning to play the James Bond theme for the performance part of his GCSE exam. I enquired why he thought he was making so little progress. I was almost totally disarmed by his honest reply: 'Because I never do any practice sir.'

The most memorable, though, has to be a teenage girl, who I was certain wasn't practising. When I challenged her about it she said I was being totally unfair and that she was practising every day but simply found learning the piano very difficult. She was so convincing that I apologised, deciding I must have misjudged the situation.

However, a week or so later, her mother rang to ask me to send her another invoice as she had lost the original. Her parting comment was: 'How can I get my daughter to practice? She doesn't go near the piano from one week to the next.'

The girl gave up the piano very shortly afterwards and I decided she had a promising future as either an actress or a politician!

Friday night is music night

In 1953 the BBC began broadcasting what has since become the world's longest running live orchestral music programme – 'Friday Night is Music Night'. If I'm in the car I sometimes catch part of it on my way home from choir practice and it always brings back lots of memories for me.

My first job on leaving school was as a music library assistant for the BBC in London. In the mid-70s it was based (along with BBC Radio 3) in a building that had been a former car showrooms, just off Great Portland Street. My job was to issue orchestral scores and parts to the various BBC orchestras for studio recordings and concerts. I was also expected to deputise for the librarian to the BBC Concert Orchestra when he was away.

In those days the recordings were, more often than not, at The Hippodrome Theatre in Golders Green and my job on arrival was to lay out all the music in the correct running order on the stands.

Sadly, I don't think I ever really enjoyed one of those concerts: That had nothing to do with the music they played, which was absolutely wonderful - but everything to do with my fear that I would be asked to transpose a part for, say, E flat saxophone, and be found wanting. Although I had only recently passed my music 'A'-level, my knowledge of the keys required for the various transposing instruments was in those days hazy to say the least.

It was an interesting job and I had to deal with requests from musicians such as John Eliot Gardiner and the late Richard Hickox, who were then at the start of what were to become very successful conducting careers.

The post was generally filled by what would nowadays be termed 'gap year' students and I inherited a huge backlog of paperwork that hadn't been dealt with by my predecessors. I have to admit that it took very little effort on my part to make inroads into this and I still somewhere have a letter from the head librarian saying I was the most efficient person who had ever worked in the post!

Sense of direction

One of the things my wife has had to learn to cope with over the time we have been married is my rather unreliable sense of direction.

It's a trait that I shared with my late brother Tim. Some years ago we had arranged to meet for a day out in Farnham, Surrey (where our parents grew up) and as my eldest daughter Katie was learning to drive and had the day free I suggested she came with me for driving practice.

We met my brother at Farnham railway station and went in search of the house where my grandfather had lived, which, amazingly, we located. But it was on our return to Farnham that things went awry. Tim and I were sure that we knew a shortcut back to the town centre - but we instead ended up in the back of beyond with poor Katie driving along narrow single-track country lanes and eventually emerged 30 minutes later near Alton, some 10 miles away from our destination.

However, I can truly claim that the occasion I got lost on a trip to play the organ at Hordle Church was not my fault.

I had been at St Thomas' a few months and the organist at Hordle asked if I would come and play as part of a music and flowers weekend they were holding. He told me that I would find the church easily once I arrived there as it was signposted.

I followed the sign and drove up and down the road several times unable to see the church. I then got out and searched on foot, even trying one or two tracks to see if the church was down there. Eventually I drove back to the crossroads and spotted a man walking his dog. On enquiry I found the church was in the opposite direction. He told me that the sign was wrong - apparently the local youngsters were often swivelling it round on the pole as a prank!

You want what….

The future of our public libraries has been a topic for much discussion in recent years, due to the cutbacks in public expenditure required to balance the nation's books.

It is certainly a service for which I am very grateful, as, despite amassing a seemingly ever-growing collection of music, there is always something I am required to play that I don't have.

Funerals and thanksgiving services are mostly necessarily arranged at short notice and it is on such occasions that I am grateful that Southampton Central Library still has a large collection of sheet music of all types.

These days a church organist can find himself being asked to play almost anything: In the last few years some of the more unusual requests have included the music for the BBC 'Test Match Special' programme and 'Always look on the bright side of life' (from the Monty Python film 'The Life of Brian').

The internet, of course, now provides a valuable resource as well. For one funeral I was asked to play 'Bless this house'. There was no copy in the library and although I remembered Harry Secombe singing it when I was younger, I couldn't remember the whole of the melody. Unable to purchase a copy in time for the service, I luckily found a video of an American organist playing it on 'YouTube' and was able to work it out from there.

A rather closer call came many years ago (in pre-internet days) when I was asked to play a traditional Scottish tune I was unable to find anywhere. I was resigned to failure, but just before the service I happened to mention it to someone who knew it and whistled me the first 8 bars. Not knowing the rest, I padded it out with a bit of the theme tune from the film 'Ice Cold in Alex', which had been shown on the television a couple of days before. Fortunately, no one seemed to notice!

Thank you Mr Phillips

I'm very lucky to work as accompanist with Philip Daish-Handy, who is one of the country's top young cellists.

As well as singing bass in our choir at St Thomas' (whenever his busy performing schedule permits) we regularly give concerts together, perform as guest entertainers on P&O cruise ships and to date have recorded three CDs

Shortly before our first recording in 2015 I was involved in a serious motorcycle accident and I clearly recall laying on a backboard in the casualty department of Southampton General Hospital: I couldn't move any of my fingers and I was left very worried that I would be ever able to play again professionally or even for fun, let alone record a CD.

That I have been able to do so is thanks to the skills of a very clever surgeon, Mr Phillips, who repaired my smashed wrist. He informed me afterwards that knowing my profession and how vital the operation was to my future he used a well-known internet site to watch pianists and how their hands and wrists moved while playing the keyboard. How lucky that we have such dedicated surgeons.

Of course, I was also overwhelmed by all the loving support and prayer I received: I understand that despite the lateness of the hour, while I was still in A & E a number of prayer groups, around the country and even in the United States went into action.

It also, I might add, took a good many hours of concentrated practice to get my left hand operating at a level somewhere near to where it was before the accident.

We chose Beaulieu Abbey for that recording session as it has a very fine Yamaha concert grand piano and is set in a quiet location. Even then, we had problems with the microphones picking up birdsong and visitors chattering outside the door: My wife Maureen also had the rather tricky task of ensuring my music pages were turned completely silently, especially as one of the microphones was less than a foot away from the music!

How the piano kept me dry

Like most musicians, I am greatly indebted to my parents for finding the money to spare to pay for my instrumental lessons, but I recall that a valuable part of my training had nothing to do with the formal tuition I received.

In fact, it came about as a result of a suggestion from an older lad in the church choir I sang in as a boy. I had been delivering newspapers six mornings a week for about a year when he suggested that I instead looked for a job like the one he had playing for ballet lessons.

My mother spotted an advert in the local paper and I went along for an audition which I managed to pass: I don't think they can have been too choosy… So, I swapped earning £1 for delivering papers in all weathers for £3 for a couple of two-hour sessions in the reasonably warm surroundings of a rather decrepit church hall and a school classroom.

It was really good training for sight reading because you were always playing music you hadn't seen before: The teachers weren't too bothered if you sounded like Les Dawson, as long as the rhythm was correct (They had a more accomplished adult pianist who played for exams and performances).

My wife Maureen had ballet lessons at the same dance school and like me can remember just what it was like. It was the early 1970s and one of the teachers demonstrated to her pupils wearing platform boots and holding a cigarette which would leave little piles of ash all over the floor!

Senior moment

One of the parts of my job as a freelance organist that I greatly enjoy is recital work, and from time to time I'm fortunate enough get asked by colleagues to play the instrument at their church. Generally I know the organ, so there are no surprises in store - unlike an organist writing in my much valued copy of 'Tales of Organists' (published 1927).

H Percy Richardson FRCO ARCM warned of the need to have as much information as possible when agreeing to play at a strange church. He wrote: 'Having been engaged to give a recital at a certain place not very far from Leeds, I arrived in the afternoon to have some little time at the organ prior to the recital in the evening.

'The tuner, who had been in the morning, left a card for me on the music desk on which he had written "You have my deepest sympathy!".'

Some years ago a friend asked me to give a lunchtime recital at his church, as part of a music festival to raise funds for various charities. The organ is a modern electronic one and makes a very good sound, thanks to the excellent acoustics of the church. The day of the recital arrived and all went without a hitch – or so I thought.

I had emailed my friend the programme of music I was going to play, but on the day I worked from my original handwritten list. On the way out, I happened to pick up the programme and noticed it contained a piece that I hadn't played! When I sent the email, I must have added the missing piece and forgotten to put it on my list.

The audience were far too polite to mention it. But it left me realising that I had just experienced one of those 'senior moments'…

Throw it away…..

Experts on television lifestyle programmes are always telling us to de-clutter our homes - and when in 2016 we moved from a roomy Victorian house in Southampton to a bungalow at Totton still undergoing major renovation and alteration, it was something I had cause to think about most carefully.

We had a large bookcase made to house all our books, but the main problem was (and continues to be) finding room to store all my music. A temporary solution was the hire of a storage unit about three miles away, where I put all the music that I felt I was very unlikely to require in the short term.

Those aforementioned experts generally advise that if you haven't needed something in the past couple of years you won't miss it. However, I had to make several visits to the storage unit to retrieve pieces of music requested for a couple of funerals and a wedding. In fact, I hadn't played any of the pieces for about 10 years and would otherwise probably have placed them in the disposal pile.

I remember some years ago receiving a phone call from a firm of undertakers the night before a funeral telling me that the deputy French ambassador would be attending the service and so I would be required to play the Marseillaise. It was too late to go to the library and the internet wasn't the default option it is now.

Luckily for me I had kept an old piano album belonging to my late father-in-law that contained all the national anthems played at the 1948 Olympic Games in London. Many of the countries have since disappeared or been renamed and I had several times considered throwing it out, but fortunately I hadn't. So, you see, the unlikeliest things can come in handy…

I am so lucky.

As I write, the 21st anniversary of my appointment as organist at St Thomas' has been and gone, and in that time I reckon (at a rough guess) I've driven nearly 120,000 miles travelling between my home in Southampton (and now Totton) and Lymington.

People often ask me how I have managed it, but to be quite honest the journey has mostly been a pleasure: My wife Maureen and I frequently reflect on how blessed we are to drive through the beautiful New Forest and see it through the changing seasons. Also, there are churches on the opposite side of Southampton to where we live which would take just as long to reach and the trip would be nowhere near as pleasant.

There is always something different to see, and mostly I am driving in the opposite direction to much of the traffic. During the summer, it is often wise to take an alternative route via Beaulieu, and for funerals and weddings one needs to allow plenty of extra time just in case.

One Christmas the wind and rain meant that we did wonder whether we would get to church on one or two occasions: The main road was flooded at Brockenhurst and only just passable when we travelled down for carol singing on Christmas Eve morning. On another occasion we had a rather longer journey home than usual when my old motorcycle – a 1961 BSA – broke its drive chain coming into Lyndhurst. But lots of kind people stopped to offer us help and we discovered that the breakdown recovery service provided by my insurers was very efficient indeed.

After one Choral Evensong a few years ago, I stupidly managed to lock the keys in the boot of my wife's little red sports car. However, we were most fortunate that the vicar came to our aid and loaned us his car, so we could drive home and fetch the spare key.

Themes from the classics

At a funeral some years ago I was asked to play the pop song 'You raise me up', which I soon realised is partly based on the old Irish tune the 'Londonderry Air' – and that set me thinking about other popular music based on or inspired by themes from the classical repertoire.

As unlikely as it seems, 'A groovy kind of love', one of the hit songs from the 1988 film 'Buster', the story of the Great Train Robbers, is based on an 18th century piano piece. The melody is sung much more slowly, but it is instantly recognisable to anyone who has studied the Rondo from Muzio Clementi's Sonatina in G major (op. 36, no. 5).

When I began playing for weddings in the 1970s 'A whiter shade of pale' by Procol Harum was a frequent request. Some years ago several of the band members got involved in a legal dispute over who had written the tune, but little was made of the fact that the whole thing is based on J S Bach's 'Air from the Suite in D' - made famous by adverts for a certain brand of cigar!

Going back to the early 1960s, when I was a little boy, Elvis Presley's song 'Can't help falling in love' was very popular. However, it was based on the melody 'Plaisir d'amour', written by Giovanni Martini in 1784.

Of course, there are many more examples and it's not just a modern phenomenon - composers have been happy to re-use tunes written by others for centuries. It just goes to show the truth of verse 9 from chapter 1 of the book of Ecclesiastes: 'There is nothing new under the sun'...

Bringing the car into the church

My job finds me playing for funerals in lots of different places and on one occasion I was asked to play in a Southampton church that I don't often visit: The organ is high up in a small gallery on the south side of the building and as I glanced in the mirror provided so the organist can see what is going on downstairs, I was momentarily transported back to the 1970s…

The reason for this was that I realised I was looking in the rear view mirror from a Hillman Avenger, a type of car that I drove for several years when I was a trainee journalist. And this later set me thinking about the various car parts I've spotted in organ consoles over the years.

The church where I was first organist for many years had console lights above the keys which were in fact Lucas car rear number plate lamps. The electric action which connected the keys to the pipes on the other side of the church operated at 16 volts, and these lamps had 16 volt bulbs to suit. When one of these eventually failed it proved very difficult to replace, so I eventually settled on a 24 volt bulb from a lorry as the car bulbs I tried blew very quickly.

At St Mary's Church in Southampton, the console has similar lamps (sadly no longer working), which could be dimmed with a rheostat switch from an old Smiths car heater.

It also has Willis 'infinite speed and gradation' swell pedals. These return to a central position when released and so an indicator to show the position of the shutters is essential. The organ builder's solution was a pair of 1950s car fuel gauges: When the boxes are open they register 'full', and when shut they read 'empty'!

Confusion over letters

My job as a freelance musician means I spend quite a bit of time at home teaching and practising and as a result I get interrupted by a lot of phone calls from people trying to sell me things that I neither want nor require.

I've signed up to the telephone preference service, but that doesn't seem to have made much difference. The obvious answer would be to go ex-directory - but that would result in me losing a lot of work, so I have to put up with it.

However, I have recently had a spate of calls from people enquiring whether I can supply them with protective overalls and workmen's boots...

It seems that my music diplomas (ARCO LTCL) have been confused by the plethora of new directory enquiry services that now exist with a firm called Arco, a leading supplier of industrial work wear and safety equipment!

There's an organ where?

Several years ago my wife spotted an article about a redundant church in the Netherlands which had been converted into a bookshop, complete with the original pipe organ. Bookworms in Zwolle can now enjoy three floors of shopping in the former Broerenkerk.

Planners set strict conditions which meant the conversion had to be done in such a way that the 550-year-old building could be returned to its previous condition if required. The architects came up with the radical redesign by using a free-standing temporary structure which includes a restaurant, but retains all the Baroque splendour of the building, including the original stained-glass window, magnificent pipe organ and ornate decoration.

Here in Britain, since the passing of the cinema organ age, we tend to think of the organ purely as a church or concert hall instrument - but there are organs to be found in some surprising places.

In the United States there is an organ in the former Wanamaker department store (now a branch of Macy's) in Philadelphia. Located in the vast shop's grand court, it boasts no less than 6 keyboards and 28,000 pipes and is the largest operational pipe organ in the world. Free recitals are still held twice every day, except on Sundays. However, my former organ teacher once played it and told me he felt it was something of a curiosity and not a particularly satisfying musical experience.

The reception hall of the Loisir Hotel Naha in Okinawa, Japan, contains a splendid looking pipe organ, while the Hoffmann organ company in Ostheim, Rhön, Germany, built an organ in the back of a lorry in 1998, which is played outside churches which don't have organs.

With two manuals and 38 ranks of pipes, the organ is cushioned from damage while the vehicle is on the move by a self-levelling air suspension system. The pipes are also provided with special shields so they don't get blocked with insects!

The salmon man

Some years ago now my wife and I were on a summer holiday in Newlyn, Cornwall, and decided to attend the Sunday morning service at the local church.

A visiting deputy organist was playing, and not recognising his concluding voluntary I had a word with him afterwards to ask who had composed it. He told me it was by 'The Salmon Man'...

Upon further enquiry I discovered it was a postlude by the organist and composer John E West, and the similarity of his name to a well-known brand of tinned fish had resulted in the nickname used by my new organist friend!

John Ebenezer West (1863-1929) was a nephew of the eminent Victorian Bach scholar Ebenezer Prout. Prout was a professor at the Royal Academy of Music and wrote many music theory books; his 1902 edition of Handel's Messiah is still in print today.

West was first taught the organ by his father, William, and later received lessons from Frederick Bridge, organist at Westminster Abbey. He studied composition at the Royal Academy of Music and in 1893 passed the fellowship exam of the College of Organists (it didn't become 'Royal' until 1893).

He held various organ posts in the London area and was conductor of several choirs and choral societies. He joined Novello as an associate editor in 1884, becoming their chief music editor and adviser in 1897.

As well as being a prolific composer himself, he produced editions of major choral works, including Brahms' Requiem, and also made a piano duet arrangement of Elgar's Enigma Variations. He died aged 65 in February 1929 after collapsing on stage at Westminster Central Hall.

Organs and Water

Over the years I must have played hundreds of different concluding voluntaries, but I recall that the piece I performed at one Epiphany Eucharist resulted in enquiries from concerned members of the congregation as to whether the organ had developed a fault...

Although unwanted notes (known as 'cyphers') are one of the hazards of being a pipe organ player, on this occasion the continuous high-pitched note above the music was deliberate.

I was playing 'Marche des Rois Mages' (March of the Magi Kings) by the French organist Théodore Dubois (1837-1924) and the high note – produced by placing a lead weight on one of the keys – is supposed to represent the star leading the wise men to Bethlehem.

The organ is a complicated instrument. Even the smallest has hundreds of moving parts, and damp, dust and even heat can quite easily cause a malfunction.

At St Thomas' the organ has a device which in dry conditions injects a fine water-spray into the winding system to maintain as far as possible the correct humidity levels for things to function properly. Nevertheless, at certain times of year one or two of the ranks of pipes have a tendency to develop 'murmurs'; quiet droning sounds caused by a small amount of air leaking past the valve which admits wind to the pipe, enabling it to speak. Fortunately, they are generally only audible if the stop concerned is drawn.

However, one very dry Easter in the early 1990s, the instrument at my previous church in Southampton developed so many murmurs that they were audible above full organ - making it unusable.

As the instrument didn't have a humidifier the organ tuner said the only answer was to place lots of pans of water inside the organ case and wait for the humidity to rise.

But as well as being very dry, the weather (and the church) was also very cold and so the organ would have remained unusable for far too long.

I gave the matter some thought and came up with the idea of placing the spout of a boiling electric kettle next to the air intake. About three kettles of water later the unwanted sounds had gone. The high temperature of the steam temporarily put one or two stops out of tune, but at least most of the organ was working in time for the Easter services!

The Speed of music

I don't get to listen to Choral Evensong on Radio 3 often enough, and on the occasions that I do hear it I am generally in the car and come in part way through the broadcast. Having not heard which cathedral or college is singing the service, I try to see if I can guess where the programme is coming from. Vast buildings such as St Paul's or Liverpool cathedrals are fairly easy to pinpoint, due to the reverberation and the slower speed at which they take they hymns to allow for this.

In parish churches these days hymns are generally taken at a 'good old lick', but it wasn't always so. In the original English Hymnal (published in 1906) musical editor Ralph Vaughan Williams suggests very slow tempos for some of the hymns: If we sang 'Holy, holy, holy' at 42 beats per minute I rather suspect people might be tempted to walk out...

When I was a young lad my first choirmaster was of the old school and took most hymns at rather sedate speeds. It certainly tested the breath capacity of the boy treble allocated to sing the first verse of 'Once in Royal David's City'.
On the other hand, hymns are occasionally sung rather too fast. I clearly remember a broadcast from an Oxford college some years ago in which the final hymn was sung so quickly that it sounded as if the choir were in a rush to catch a bus.

Maureen and I were at the annual dinner of the Winchester Organists' Association a few years ago, when the guest speaker was one of our local cathedral organists. He gave a very amusing talk in which he said that his cathedral was noted for singing hymns rather faster than others. He explained that this was because of his experience as a teenager. Apparently, at the first ever service for which he played the organ, the priest announced the second hymn with the words 'and can we sing it rather faster than the last one please'!

Why we wear cassocks

Every year members of our choir at St Thomas' have the opportunity to sing with other choirs from around the Diocese at the annual Royal School of Church Music Festival at Winchester Cathedral. And no matter how many choirs are taking part, I can always spot our choristers amongst all the other singers due to the distinctive terracotta colour of their robes.

People sometimes ask why we wear robes. In fact, it stems from a long tradition dating back to early Christian times when choirs began to adopt clothing based on the ancient tunic, which was the model for clerical vestments.

Firstly, cassocks or robes are if you like the choir's 'work clothes', denoting the special task they have to perform in helping lead the music of our worship.

They also provide uniformity so that people aren't distracted by what choir members may be wearing: Secular choirs generally have some sort of 'uniform' as well, to prevent audience members having their attention diverted from the music by someone wearing a brightly coloured dress or shirt.

Thirdly, they help reinforce the importance of teamwork. A good church choir has to learn to work efficiently together just as much as any football or sports team.

One further benefit, particularly in churches that don't have good heating, can be the warmth they help provide. As a little boy, I was always glad of my cassock and surplice as the church where I sang was extremely cold - so cold, in fact, that in the winter my choirmaster used to wear his organists' surplice (properly known as a 'winged rochet') over the top of his duffel coat!

Cinema organists

Back in 2012, the enormous success of the French silent film, The Artist, in the BAFTA and Oscar awards set me thinking about the origins of organ music at the cinema.

In the early days of film it was often the job of a pianist to interpret what he saw and provide an instant musical accompaniment to the on-screen action. Indeed, my wife's late foster father, who was a music teacher in Hove in the 1920s and 30s, supplemented his income from teaching and playing the organ in church by playing at a local cinema.

As film became more popular organs which featured all sorts of orchestral and special effects, including sirens, drums and bird whistles, were installed in many cinemas. However the arrival of the 'talkie' meant they were quite soon relegated to entertaining the audience between films and during the intermission.

My first visit to the cinema as a small boy was to see a black and white film 'The Wrong Arm of the Law', starring Peter Sellers. Although there were plenty of cinemas in Southampton, we went to 'The Regal' at Eastleigh because my father enjoyed listening to the organ, which in those days was still in use there.

The job of cinema organist involved a high degree of skill in improvisation (making music up on the spot) and is only something that organists and jazz musicians are generally expected to do. One of the world's top improvisers is David Briggs, who began his career as organist at Gloucester Cathedral, and now makes his living as a concert organist. He regularly improvises amazing pieces in several movements on a theme submitted by a member of the audience. And in recent years he has revived the cinema organist's art by accompanying live showings of old silent films.

My Bach was much worse than my bite!

Danger and adventure are hardly things you would associate with practicing a musical instrument, but learning the organ can sometimes prove a perilous business...

Firstly, you have to gain access to an instrument; nearly always in a church and, unlike St. Thomas, Lymington, more than often locked. As a schoolboy I frequently had to cycle several miles in search of a keyholder (who was at home) to gain entry to the building.

Then there's the location of the instruments themselves. I remember one organ where the player had to ascend a flight of stairs and a rickety wooden ladder to gain access to the console, high up on a wall. And, truth to tell, it was hardly worth the effort.

While working in London in the mid-1970s I was fortunate enough to be given permission to practice on the fabulous Henry Willis grand organ in Westminster RC Cathedral. I arrived shortly after 7pm and was shown up to the west end gallery. I was told to play quietly until the visitors left at 7.30pm. at 7.25pm I looked in the mirror and saw one or two people still walking around. When I next looked, all I saw was pitch blackness, except for a small lamp in the organ loft – and I had no torch with me.

Determined not to waste the opportunity, I played for about two hours before plucking up the courage to 'feel' my way along a side gallery and make my exit via a staircase at the east end of the cathedral that led to the clergy house (street level) and the crypt...Luckily I found the right door.

However, my biggest fright came a few years later while I was practicing hard for a diploma examination at the church where I was organist in Millbrook, Southampton. I was in the habit of playing every evening after work and would often launch straight into a very loud passage of the piece I was working on.

One evening I entered the church and knowing the layout of the building I only switched on the south aisle lights to get to the organ. I started playing a rather loud piece of Bach, to warm my fingers up when I heard a noise which seemed to emanate from the choir vestry and sacristy, on the opposite of the church.

Without putting on any more illumination I went into the gloom of the darkened sacristy and saw tramp helping himself to a box of communion wine. I was so shocked that I let him run past me and out of the door. Thinking back on it, I think he was probably terrified as the sound of full organ (the pipes situated very close to the sacristy) must have made him think that his theft was being met by divine retribution!

Music fashion

Fashion is not something confined to the latest styles in clothing or cars – hymns are every bit as subject to changes in tastes and attitudes as the years roll by. Although 'All things bright and beautiful' is still a very popular hymn, no modern hymn book contains the verse 'The rich man in his castle, the poor man at his gate; God made them, high or lowly, and ordered their estate'. And yet it was still to be found in the old 'Ancient and Modern' until the revised version appeared in 1950.

Many hymns have been more subtly altered, with the removal of such words as 'heathen', which are no longer considered acceptable. Others have simply disappeared: When I was a choirboy we regularly sang William's Cowper's communion hymn 'There is a fountain filled with blood, drawn from Emmanuel's veins', which was in the old English Hymnal. But it is not to be found in either our own Ancient and Modern New Standard or the New English Hymnal.

Two we never sang (but whose words I found fascinating) were: 'Who is this with garments gory, Triumphing from Bozrah's way'; and 'The world is very evil, the times are waxing late; be sober and keep vigil, The judge is at the gate'. However, the editors of the English Hymnal must have thought them to be useful when the book was first published in 1906.

As I've mentioned before, one of my favourite hymns – again not found in many modern hymn books – is 'Nearer my God to thee', reputed to have been played by the musicians on board the Titanic as the liner sank in April 1912. I like to think it was J B Dykes' wonderful tune 'Horbury', and I was saddened to hear the American tune used when the film 'Titanic' came out in 1997. It is perhaps difficult to know which tune they played – but the memorial to them, near London Road, in Southampton, is inscribed with the melody of Dykes' tune.

Manuscript rules

Just as in every other walk of life, computers are making vast inroads into the everyday lives of musicians. In my case I enter my pupils for exams online and produce my annual accounts using computer spreadsheets: even some of the organs I am regularly asked to play are digital and run by computer chip.

However, when it comes to writing out music I still cling to the tried and trusted method of using a pencil and manuscript paper. My younger colleagues use computer-based programmes to produce some very nice looking printed parts, but it can be a very time consuming business and I find it much easier and quicker to write them out by hand.

Running a junior school orchestra, I am always having to produce simplified parts or transpose an existing part into a different key for instruments such as the E flat tenor horn, which are not found in the run of the mill junior orchestra sets.

Over the years I have found myself transposing a number of songs into a higher key for my youngest daughter Libby – and I also had to produce a piano transcription from an orchestral score for a lunchtime recital I was giving with a singer.

The manuscript pads I purchased from my local music store are ideal except for one problem – the staves are printed on expensive looking shiny paper which makes the music written on them virtually illegible under bright lights. The way round this, however, is to photocopy the music on plain paper.

I still marvel at the vast quantities of music composers such as J S Bach wrote in an age when the music lines had first to be ruled on to the page before any notes could be written down. I've no doubt this was a job given to pupils and assistants – but perhaps he would have been as sceptical about manuscript pads as I am about modern computer-based systems!

Fashions in organ music

The world of the organ and organ music, like many things in life, is very much subject to the whims of fashion.

When I began lessons at the start of the 1970s what is known as the 'organ reform' movement was still in the ascendancy. This was in crude terms a 'back to basics' approach to organ design and construction and the performance of its repertoire.

Recitals with works all by one composer were in vogue and music by organists such as Josef Rheinberger and Percy Whitlock – which had been very popular before the Second World War – was often ignored.

Fortunately, the wheel has turned almost full circle during the past 30 to 40 years and the current generation of performers are quite happy to play worthwhile music from all periods and styles.

The reform movement did bring many benefits, however, not least in that it led to a more informed approach to the performance of early music and the rediscovery of much repertoire from the 17th and 18th centuries, which in its own turn had been largely ignored by many 19th and early 20th century players.

English organs were among the last in Europe to adopt pedals and so organists were at first reluctant to play the wealth pieces by John Stanley (1713 – 86), the blind organist of London's Temple Church, and his contemporaries, in their original 'manuals only' form. Clumsy arrangements were made, adding almost virtuosic pedal parts and filling out the harmony with thick chords.

The sounds made by organs at this time were also changing and stops such as the Cornet – a distinctive solo colour made from several ranks of pipes sounding together – were dispensed with. Nowadays I find that the Cornet Voluntaries by John Stanley and others, with their display of rapid right-hand passagework, are always very popular with listeners. However, a book on organ design and construction by J W Hinton (published in 1910 – the year before the organ at St Thomas' was installed) has the following to say about the Cornet:

'The Cornet was used for giving out psalm tunes and for a particularly detestable form of voluntary, now, happily, obsolete.'!

Best seat in the house, or is it?

Playing the organ in St Thomas' I reckon I have one of the 'best seats in the house'. From the console in the west-end gallery I can clearly see the high altar, the choir stalls and the pulpit - and thanks to the lovely new glass entrance doors I can even see what's going on in the narthex via a discreet mirror.

However, the one part of the building I can't see is the Courtenay Chapel. I was reminded of this when playing for a thanksgiving service recently and I was very glad to have our verger Joan Townley on hand to tell me when to begin playing and when to stop.

In many churches, the organ is crammed into a dark corner and the organist may not even have eye contact with the choir.

At Southwark Cathedral the organ console is on the north side of the choir and for many years the organist sat with his back to the singers, looking at the conductor in a mirror through a gap in the choir screen. No doubt these days the organist has some sort of hi-tech CCTV system to give him or her a much better view.

Before the war it wasn't the custom for cathedral choirs to have a conductor and they had to keep in time with the organ, perhaps getting a beat from one of the choir men. If my memory serves me correct, I believe that at King's College, Cambridge, there was many years ago some sort of mechanical arm which the organist could operate to indicate the beat.

But I will never forget my surprise at seeing a telephone in the organ console at a large Roman Catholic Church in Wimbledon, where I played for a school end of term service in the early 1980s. The Church of the Sacred Heart is of cathedral proportions and the choir and organ are in a west-end gallery at a far distance from the high altar. The organ console, which is in the main case of the instrument, faces west and so a telephone system with a red flashing light instead of a ring-tone had been installed so that the clergy could keep in touch with the organist.

Pipe verses organ

Spending part of a summer Bank Holiday Monday afternoon fixing a push lawnmower that Maureen and I had only purchased the previous autumn set me thinking about the longevity of many of the pipe organs I meet in my work as a 'jobbing' organist.

Two days before I was playing for a wedding at a Southampton church which has a one manual organ built by J W Walker and Sons in 1857, and still works remarkably well, despite the fact that it hasn't had vast sums of money spent on it. In fact, it is an interesting instrument in that it has a 'dumb organist'. This device (one of only a two or three known to survive) can be placed over the keys to play a selection of hymns by turning a handle.

Then there was the organ at All Saints' Church, Lymington, (now closed for worship) which I used to play regularly for weddings and funerals. It was installed in 1909 (when it may well have been second-hand) and had had scarcely anything done to it other than tuning ever since.

A friend of mine was until fairly recently organist at a church near Southampton which has a marvellous Father Willis organ dating from 1872. It was rescued from a bombed out school chapel in London just after the second world war and apart from a clean and overhaul in the 1980s has been giving excellent service for over 65 years.

Many churches faced with the cost of repairing and maintaining a pipe organ have been forced by economic circumstances to replace them with an electronic substitute. However, like our lawnmower, they are not always such a good buy: I know of one church which purchased a fairly expensive electronic instrument in the 1990s and is now having to replace it because it is giving so much trouble.

The importance of the apostrophe

I'm not a great fan of modern hi-tech gadgets, but I must admit I have come to find emails and text messages very useful in organising my working life.

However, one of the things that has suffered as a result of these modern forms of communication is most definitely punctuation, and I am often reminded how important commas and full stops are in imparting the correct meaning when rehearsing hymns with our choir at St Thomas'.

Possibly the most popular of all metrical psalms is the translation of Psalm 23 sung to the tune of 'Crimond', 'The Lord's my shepherd, I'll not want': Yet one so often hears it performed without the comma, making complete nonsense of the meaning of the words.

As a small boy I was always rather bemused by George Herbert's last verse in 'King of glory, King of peace', which begins, 'Seven whole days, not one in seven, I will praise thee'. Being too young to appreciate the punctuation I used to think to myself: 'Surely we can be allowed to praise God at least once a week?'

My young self also misunderstood Mrs Alexander's hymn 'There is a green hill far away'. Forget the fact that our Lord was almost certainly crucified on the local rubbish tip, I thought for a long time that it was a hill without a wall, not a hill outside of the city wall.

Possibly the biggest howler, however, was the original translation from the German in the well-known Easter hymn 'Jesus lives!'. In the old edition of the Ancient and Modern, which was still in frequent use up until the 1960s, the first line ran: 'Jesus lives no longer now'. Of course, I've missed out the all-important exclamation mark to make my point...

Pedals – the new addition!

Like most instruments of its type, the chamber organ I am lucky to have, as well as the main organ, to use to accompany the choir during services has no pedals.

It has provided me with a good opportunity to occasionally explore music for 'manuals only' for my voluntaries – as, without pedals most of the standard repertoire by Bach, Mendelssohn and the 19th and 20th century French composers has been 'off the menu'.

Although organs in Northern Germany had what we would recognise as a pedal organ by the early 1600, pedals didn't arrive in England until rather later.

The organ in St. Paul's Cathedral is thought to have been the first and gained some pedals during the 1720s. according to the organist, Dr Greene, Handel liked to play there ' for exercise it offered him in the use of the pedals'.

In fact, it was to be another seventy or eighty years before pedals were anything like commonplace on English organs, and then they were generally rather crude devices that acted as 'pull-downs' for the manual stops rather than being separate pedal divisions in their own right.

By the time of the Great Exhibition of 1851, all leading English organ builders were producing instruments with proper pedals. However, there were not embraced enthusiastically by every player. Seventy-five year old Sir George Smart, organist of the Chapel Royal, turned down the offer to try one of the new instruments with the following riposte: 'My dear Sir, I have never in my life played on a gridiron' ……

Pianola – no practice required!

Modern electric keyboards and digital pianos generally have a 'demo' button that enables the instrument to play a number of selected pieces itself - but this is not an entirely new idea.

I used to be regularly reminded of this fact when our usual Friday night choir practice was relocated to our former daughter church All Saints' because of an event being held in St Thomas'. The old upright piano there was originally a pianola, but most of the self-playing mechanism was removed many years ago, leaving it to play as a normal acoustic instrument.

On closer inspection, however, some of the control levers could still be found under a hinged rail in front of the keyboard, and the pedals which would have pneumatically driven the punched paper 'piano rolls' placed inside were still behind a fold-down panel at the bottom of the case.

It was built by the London firm of Sir Herbert Marshall and Rose, probably in the 1920s or early 30s. Founded in 1907, they were relative latecomers to the pianola craze, which lasted from the late 1890s until the mid-1920s. The first pianolas were expensive pieces of kit, costing the equivalent of over £4,000 in today's money. But later on, cheaper models were launched and by the time sales peaked in 1924 more than half of all pianos sold in America contained a player unit. Five years later, following the stock market crash of 1929 and the rapid development of gramophone records, their day had passed - although one or two companies struggled on until the end of the 1930s.

Curiously, there is still a firm that manufactures piano rolls and can supply thousands of titles from stock. Also, if you search the internet, you can hear the great French impressionist composer Claude Debussy playing the piano via a recording of a pianola roll which he made in Paris in 1913.

Importance of piano tuning

Although my first instrument is the organ, I spend much more of my time playing the piano - giving lessons to pupils, accompanying singers and instrumentalists or simply leading choir rehearsals. Concert pianists have their choice of the top Steinway and Yamaha grand pianos and some even tour with their own instrument, but as a 'jobbing' pianist one has to be able to make do with whatever is available.

At St Thomas' we are fortunate to have a fine Blüthner grand piano in the church and a very good digital (electric) piano in the hall.

However, this is certainly not the case in every place. Some years ago now a school choir I work with had been asked to sing Christmas carols at a private hospital. I had been told there was a Bechstein grand piano for me to play. But when we got there we discovered it pushed against a very hot central heating radiator which had cracked the soundboard; and from the state of the case it looked as though it had been dropped down several flights of stairs. I had to play it as there wasn't anything else available - and yes, it sounded absolutely dreadful…

On another occasion I was playing for a friend's Christmas concert. The upright piano in the little country church didn't sound too bad during the rehearsal: A low note was jammed, but I could play round it. About half way through the programme, however, I lost every note in the bottom half of the keyboard. My friend's face when I began the introduction for the next piece playing it two octaves higher than written was a picture!

Old music copies

Much of my organ music has been inherited from people over the years and as a consequence some of it is rather tatty.

However, I've grown rather fond of playing from particular copies and editions and when I perform a piece it often brings back memories of the person to whom it used to belong.

I have several books that belonged to D Cecil Williams – well known organist of St Mary's, Southampton, from the early 1930s until the late 60s. He always noted in pencil on the music when he had played a particular piece – and sometimes made other comments. One copy reads: '9/X/62 -made a mess of registration'.

Some of my oldest and most worn music belonged to an elderly gentleman whom I succeeded as organist at a small suburban church in my teens. A French master at Taunton's Grammar School in Southampton, he had a habit of writing in fountain pen on his music...

Yet more copies were inherited from my wife's father, an accomplished pianist and organist who purchased much of it from Lyon and Hall in Brighton in the 1920s and 30s.

One particular copy is in almost pristine condition and it didn't take me long to find out why. The volume in question contains Handel's organ concertos arranged for the organ by W T Best, a Victorian virtuoso player.

Most of it is completely unplayable and needs re-arranging. One particular piece contains very fast demi-semiquaver scales to be played by the feet and I have re-arranged it so that the passages in question are played by the left hand.

My justification for doing so is backed up by a story told in yet another inherited old book - 'Tales of organists', published in 1927.

One W H Bates, organist of Ash, near Aldershot, recalls hearing the following conversation with Best after a recital:

Young organist: 'Mr Best, I like your arrangements for the organ and can play them all'.

Mr Best: 'I can't'!

The 'Reluctant organist'

I recently received a letter from the local organist's association asking for help to publicise a course they were running for 'reluctant organists'.

You may be asking yourself 'what is a reluctant organist'? well, it is really the very opposite of how it sounds. A 'reluctant' is a volunteer, generally with basic piano or keyboard skills, who offers to take on the role of playing the organ and leading the music at a church when there is no one else to do so.

These days many churches find it difficult to recruit a suitable musician to lead the music at their service. It is not only due to a shortage of players, as many able musicians do not want to be tied down at weekends; hence the increasing use of teams of players in some parishes.

However, before the Second World War even small suburban parishes could often count on the services of a trained Church musician. And theatre and cinema organists such as Reginald Dixon and Sidney Torch were ranked among the best known popular musical celebrities of their day – with salaries to match.

I remember hearing Robin Richmond (the man who played fanfares on the Hammond organ on 1960s television programmes such as 'Double Your Money') interviewed on the radio some years ago.

He said that he had trained before the war by applying for a job as assistant organist at a big London cinema at the then princely sum of £15 per week. He was a church organist but was given the job anyway. He paid the organist £5 a week for lessons and another £5 to do his assistant's role – leaving him with £5 a week to live on (the same as my father was then earning as a Fleet Street reporter!)

Training methods in the major churches and cathedrals could sometimes be haphazard too. Sir Henry Walford Davies (composer of God be in my head and Solemn Melody) complained that when he was organ scholar at St. George's Chapel, Windsor in the 1890s, he received virtually no instruction or advice from the organist Sir Walter Parratt. He and fellow organ scholar Hubert Hunt were 'left to get on with it'.

Fortunately, there are plenty of training opportunities for organists today. In our parish we run an organ scholarship scheme, which has trained a number of future organists. Already previous organ scholars have helped, and are helping, in services across the country and further afield.

What's in a number?

If you've ever looked at the console of an organ you may have wondered why the stops are marked with a series of numbers, such as '16', '8', '4' and '2'.

Well the numbers refer to the relative pitches of the ranks of pipes concerned. The stops marked with an '8' sound at the same pitch as the piano and the number describes the nominal length in feet (no metric measurements here!) of the lowest sounding open pipe.

Stops marked with a '4' sound an octave (8 notes) above and with a '2', a further octave higher.

Many of the pedal stops operated by the player's feet sound at 16 foot pitch, an octave lower than the piano – and at Winchester Cathedral there are some 32 foot pipes, which sound an octave lower again. At St. Thomas' we have a pedal stop marked '32', but the sound it makes is the result of an acoustic trick (two pipes sounding together to produce the low rumbling effect).

Cast your eyes around the array of stops more closely and you may also spot further numbers such as '12', '19' and '22'. These denote the composition of 'mixture' stops, which sould several different ranks of pipes of various pitches (most often octaves and fifths) to add brilliance to the overall sound.

You may even find one or two fractions, such as 2 2/3 and 1 3/5. These are called 'mutation' stops and build on the natural harmonics present in all musical sounds to create special solo effects.

An exhibition of effectiveness

I've always had a soft spot for the French 19th century showman organist Lefébure-Wély - ever since I used one of his simpler pieces as a concluding voluntary for the very first church service I played for as a 14 year-old boy.

I started my church playing career by accident when the regular organist failed to turn up. Having no music with me, I searched the shelves of a rather dusty bookcase next to the organ and found an old book of pieces by Lefébure-Wély, one of which I managed to sight-read.

Louis James Alfred Lefébure-Wély was born in Paris in 1817, the son of a church organist. He was a child prodigy who was playing the organ in public by the age of eight. He studied at the Paris Conservatoire, winning first prize for organ in 1835. In 1847 he was appointed organist of the Madeleine in Paris. Sixteen years later he moved to St Sulpice, where he was still organist when he died in 1869 aged 52.

He was a noted improviser and his public performances always drew large crowds. He was in charge of the music for the funeral of Frédéric Chopin in 1849, and his organ transcriptions of some of Chopin's piano works were highly praised by the critics.

Lefébure-Wély's own compositions were very much influenced by the light operas that were popular in Paris at the time. As my musical dictionary notes: 'He was not oppressed by the traditional dignity of the instrument, and both his playing and his compositions exhibited brilliant immediate effectiveness'.

However, this populist approach meant that his music soon came to be considered vulgar and in poor taste. Certainly, when I was first learning the organ in the early 1970s, it was very much at odds with the prevailing tastes of the time.

Fortunately, this attitude has relaxed in recent years and his music is once again delighting many church congregations and recital audiences.

Flemish joy

Looking for something different to play at the end of the Palm Sunday morning service one year, I settled on a chorale prelude on the hymn tune 'Aberystwyth' by the Belgian organist and composer Flor Peeters.

Chorale preludes are a form of composition most commonly associated with Baroque composers such as Johann Pachelbel, Dietrich Buxtehude and Johann Sebastian Bach - but Peeters wrote about 150 of them, many based on familiar British hymn tunes.

Flor Peeters (1903 – 1986) studied at the Lemmens Institute, Mechelen, where he was appointed a professor in 1923. Later he taught at the major music institutions in Ghent, Tilburg, and Antwerp, while also pursuing a successful international career as an organ recitalist.

His music is characterised by the use of classical forms with attractively dissonant 20th century harmony, influenced by Flemish Renaissance polyphony and folk music. As well as 24 sets of chorale preludes, he wrote a number organ suites, solo pieces and a very successful tutor book 'Ars Organi', which was 'all the rage' when I began studying the organ in the early 1970s.

For my Grade 8 examination I learnt what is most probably his best known work - 'Aria' - a haunting melody written in 1946, and I have been an enthusiast of his music ever since.

Although Peeters gave some recitals in England in the 1970s, I never managed to hear him play. However, my late brother Tim met him on a European singing tour in the early 1980s and was able to tell Flor Peeters how keen his little brother was on his music!

The patent pending organ

To the casual observer, there is nothing much out of the ordinary about the organ in St. Thomas Church. From the body of the church, one can only see a rather plain wooden organ case with an unremarkable row of metal front pipes.

However, the church possesses what is almost certainly the only remaining large instrument by the once proud Sheffield firm of Brindley and Foster.

The installation of the organ was part of an extensive renovation of the church undertaken at the end of the Edwardian era. Brindley and Foster were asked to incorporate as much of the 1831 Walker instrument as possible; Indeed the old decorated front pipes now sit in the swell box at the back of the present organ.

It was built to a design unique to Brindleys, and as installed boasted four miles of lead pneumatic tubing and 1816 pipes. The lead tubing was removed when the organ was overhauled and the key action electrified at the beginning of the 1992, which must have greatly reduced the loading on the structure of the 18th century gallery!

But it is the console from which the organ is played that is of most interest from an historical point of view. In fact, when the latest overhaul work was carried out in 2005, we had to get permission to recondition the keyboards from the Council for the Care of Churches.

In 1911, the console, which unusually for the time boasted a general crescendo pedal (it gradually brings all the stops without moving the stop knobs) and special controls to give pre-set combinations of sounds, was considered of such an advanced design that it was put on display in the window of

Chappell's music shop in London before its installation at Lymington.

Brindleys registered various patents for their designs, but other organ builders chose instead to adopt a different system of stop control which is now standard on most modern organs. This left Brindley and Foster to 'plough their own furrow; as it were until the firm folded in the late 1930s and was taken over by the famous London organ builders Henry Willis and Sons.

Valuable Craftwork

Pipe organ building is an ancient craft that can be traced back to Roman times, so you would be forgiven for thinking that it has had little influence outside the religious and musical circles.

But I was surprised to read in an article in 'Organist Review', by English organ builder David Shuker, that in their endeavours to improve the instrument over the centuries, organ makers have come up with ideas and designs which have a surprising relevance to modern life – and even research into outer space!

Look at the perfectly flat surface of a table or a bookshelf and you're seeing the results of a manufacturing process originally developed by organ builders. In order to minimise the loss of wind and make the playing action light as possible, the wooden parts have to be as flat and smooth as possible; something very difficult to achieve with hand tools. Organ builders solved this as long ago as the 1700s by developing a planing machine.

On one summer holiday aboard ship Maureen and I were awoken one morning by the sound of fog-horns. Again, the basic design for these was developed by the late Victorian English organ builder Robert Hope-Jones, who was trying to develop a much louder organ pipe.

His new stop, the Diaphone, made a dreadful din and the designs was not adopted by other organ builders: However, it was discovered that the sound carried very well in dense fog and so it developed into the fog-horn.

What about outer space? Well, I won't pretend that I begin to understand it, but the French physicist Leon Faucault's experiments in the 1860s into measuring the speed of light required a complicated apparatus powered by a special set of bellows and a wind reservoir – built for him by the famous organ builder Arstide Cavaillé-Coll. Apparently, the machine is still on display in a Paris museum.

So, the skill of the pipe organ builder is perhaps something we should value rather more than we do in an age when many churches are replacing their pipe organs with cheap electronic instruments.

A poor workman blames his tools, surely?

According to the old saying a poor workman blames his tools – but in the case of some church organs, this may well be not quite fair.

At St. Thomas' we are lucky in having a far-sighted vicar and PCC who maintain the church's historic (and quite probably unique) Brindley and Foster instrument. However, there are a number of places where there is either not the will or the necessary money to do so.

If you asked a violinist to play on an instrument with a missing string or a clarinettist to play with several of the keys jammed you would almost certainly be told to think again.

But in the past 30 odd years I have worked as an organist I have been expected to play on organs which are relatively in a much worse state.

I remember one occasion when I was asked to play for a funeral in Southampton at which former BBC Antiques Roadshow presenter Hugh Scully was to read a lesson. When I arrived, I found much of the organ out of tune and had to play the pedals with the sides of my feet as the shafts of the natural keys had warn almost level with those of the sharps and flats and playing in the usual manner resulted in an unwanted 'play one and get one free' effect!

On another occasion I found myself playing a lovely old organ on which someone had mounted an elegant swan-necked brass lamp right in the middle of the music desk, so virtually nothing bigger than a hymn book could be placed on it. I had to place my music copies on the organ bench and try to play as best as I could peering over my shoulder.

However, I think the very worst experience was playing for a funeral on an ancient clapped-out electronic instrument. Try as I might I couldn't find one sound that wasn't dreadful. I was so embarrassed that I played nothing but the three hymns requested and scuttled off out of the church as fast as I could resolved never to play there again…

Armed for Tension

As organist and choir director at St Thomas' I am responsible for ensuring both organs and the grand piano are maintained in the best possible condition.

The main organ generally receives a visit from the organ builder about three times a year, when it is tuned, and any minor faults are attended to.

In the meantime, there can be the odd pipe that needs knocking back into tune or a cypher (a note that sounds when it shouldn't) that needs silencing: This falls to me, and generally I can deal with this sort of thing.

But tuning the whole instrument is a very different matter and is most definitely the province of an experienced professional.

The same applies to the piano. After one of the concerts Phil and I gave on our recent cruise, a member of the audience asked when the pianos on the ship were tuned and if I had tuned the Steinway grand on which I was lucky enough to be playing. I explained it was a job for a highly trained professional and was done each time the ship was in Southampton.

However, it reminded me of a story I was told by a retired school teacher who played the drums.

In the 1960s he and a pianist pal had landed themselves a job entertaining guests over the Christmas holiday in a country hotel. They visited a few days beforehand and found one or two notes on the piano needed tuning. His friend was quite skilled at this, but unfortunately left the tuning arm on top of the instrument…

When they returned they found a young guest had released the tension on nearly all the strings and the piano was completely unplayable!

White Out

We are very lucky to still regularly sing Choral Evensong at St Thomas', Lymington, but I'm sure the congregation are not aware that several of the choir's favourite musical settings have a link to Gloucester Cathedral.

The anthem, Blessed be the God and Father, which we often sing at Easter, was written by Samuel Sebastian Wesley, who was cathedral organist at Gloucester from 1865 to 1867 (and who visited St Thomas' Church in 1862 to play the organ).

Then there are a set of responses written by the late John Sanders, organist of Gloucester from 1976 to 1994, and a setting of the canticles, composed by another of his illustrious predecessors, Sir Alfred Herbert Brewer.

Born in 1865, Brewer was organist of Gloucester from 1896 until his death in 1928. He lived in the city his whole life and was a contemporary of Sir Edward Elgar.

His lovely D major setting of the Magnificat and Nunc Dimittis was written for the Three Choirs Festival held at Hereford in 1927, and if you search online you will find a recording of the Nunc Dimittis with orchestral accompaniment made by HMV at that very service.

Brewer transcribed several of Elgar's orchestral works for organ and one of his own pieces, March Heroique, is very much in the style of Elgar's pomp and circumstance marches.

My late brother Tim was singing at a funeral service some years ago now, at which this piece was played by one of the country's top recital organists. Afterwards, Tim happened to remark that I was struggling learning it because of the very large stretches in the right hand.

His advice was as follows: 'Tell him to do what I do old boy – get out the Tipp-Ex'!

St. Thomas Organ, Lymington, Hampshire

Brindley and Foster built in 1911

GREAT ORGAN
1. Double Open Diapason   16ft
2. Open Diapason Major   8ft
3. Open Diapason Minor   8ft
4. Harmonic Flute   8ft
5. Flute   4ft
6. Principal   4ft
7. Fifteenth   2ft
8. Twelfth   2⅔ft
9. Trumpet   8ft

SWELL ORGAN
10. Bourdon   16ft
11. Open Diapason   8ft
12. Gedact   8ft
13. Viola da Gamba   8ft
14. Voix Cèlestes   8ft
15. Flauto Magico   4ft
16. Principal   4ft
17. Mixture   3 ranks
18. Oboe   8ft
19. Clarinet   8ft
20. Horn   8ft
21. Contra Fagotto   16ft
22. Tremulant

CHOIR ORGAN
23. Gedact   8ft
24. Dulciana   8ft
25. Salicet   4ft
26. Piccolo   2ft
27. Larigot   1⅓ft
28. Clarinet (from Swell) 8ft
29. Trumpet (from Great)   8ft

PEDAL ORGAN
30. Contra-Bass   32ft
31. Open Diapason   16ft
32. Violone (from Great)   16ft
33. Soubasse   16ft
34. Bourdon (from Swell)   16ft
35. Flute   8ft
36. Cello   8ft
37. Bassoon (from Swell)   16ft

COUPLERS
1. Great to Pedal
2. Swell to Pedal
3. Choir to Pedal
4. Choir to Great
5. Choir to Swell*
6. Swell to Great
7. Swell Octave
8. Swell Sub-Octave

SOLO TRANSFORMERS
(to manuals 1, 3 and Pedal)
1. Flute Solo
2. Oboe Solo
3. Horn Solo

TRANSFORMERS
(to Swell and Pedal)
1. Viola Cèlestes
2. Flute Cèlestes
3. Woodwind
4. Orchestra
5. Chorus
6. Reeds
7. Flues

MANUAL TOUCHES
(pistons) to Great Organ
1. Diapasons   8ft
2. Flute Solo   8ft
3. Flute Solo   4ft
4. Trumpet Solo   8ft
5. Negative
6. Compound

PEDAL TOUCHES
1. Bourdon
2. Soubasse and Flute
3. Add Violone and Cello
4. Full
5. Negative

CHOIR TOUCHES
1. Dulciana
2. Add Gedact
3. Add Salicet
4. Add Piccolo
5. Negative

ACCESSORIES
1. Grand Choeur (stop giving full organ effects with couplerType equation here.s etc)
2. Free Pedal (stop cancels pre-set pedal for solo transformers)
3. Free Accompaniment (stop cancels pre-set accompaniment for solo transformers)
4. Balanced Swell Pedal
5. Reversible Great to Pedal
6. Reverser switch to enable Swell to Choir coupling*
7. Five Composition Pedals to Great and Pedal
8. Five Composition Pedals to Swell
9. General Crescendo Pedal (with indicator panel and hitchdowns for Swell/Pedal and Great/Pedal)